Poems

Israfil Sahibdeen

This book is a work of fiction. Names, characters, places, and incidents are the product of the author's imagination or are used fictitiously. Any resemblance to actual locales, events, or persons, living or dead, is purely coincidental.

Printed in the United States of America.

Page Solutions - Prowriters Network
541 Buttermilk Pike
Crescent Springs, KY 41017

ISBN: 979-8-89633-012-7 (paperback)
ISBN: 979-8-89633-013-4 (ebook)

CONTENTS

PART ONE

The Young Woman

Like a rose standing in a garden of love
Young and beautiful
Eloquent and passionate
Glowing in the sunlight –
Her beauty parades on a stage of adoration.
She brings joy to humanity.

Her charms are adorable
Her smiles are captivating
A jewel the world can see

<u>Drought</u>

The rain has ceased
angry winds pushed the dark clouds away
leaving behind the clear blue skies
the golden sun displays it's strength-
showing off its power
like a whirl wind devouring all in it's path

Seven days has gone
the heat builds –up from dust to dawn
sediments and mud left at the bottom of the pond
signs of hard-times to come.

The villagers looked to the heavens
no sign of hope
they looked in despair
"are we tasting the bitterness of hell"
they lamented with fear.
looked at each other.
"why our Lord punishing us?

As the days gone by
the heat increases
the once saturated earth
is now parched and dried
cracks like artistic designs
can be seen all over the land
"is it a land of damnation"

Plants and trees tastes the bitterness of the evil world
birds and insects struggling to survive
while skeletons of fishes lined the river beds

Villagers gathered, each in their sect
praying to their rain gods
to send the rain upon the land

They prayed day and night
chanting praises to their gods
but their gods never heard
"are our praises are in vain, for yet there is no rain"

The men harvest grains, fruits
even the young ones were collected
for not too long , they would be none.

Seven days turned to seven months
the smell off carcass traveled on the wings of the wind
no living things could have been seen-
but man – barely holding on.
for not too long
if the rain don't come
they too would be gone.

Only Once

A world of beauty
A world of sin
A world where some live together
And where others are enemies
A world of love
A world of hate
A world where some are rich
And where others are poor
A world of joy
A world of sadness
A world where man walked - but once
But never to returned.

So let us enjoy it's beauty
Let us live together
Let us embrace love
Let richness of knowledge fills our hearts
For only once-
We enjoyed its beauty
Only once –
We suffered its sins
Only once-
We are here
Only once-
Life will be gone.

The Flower

Your eyes sparkle like diamonds in the sun
Lips moist with crystal dew-drops
Your face glows with adoration
Your heart dances to the rhythm of the wind
While humming birds and bees siphon nectar from your bosom
You're the morning star –
You're the evening star –
At nighttime, you will go to bed never to return
In the morning time, your siblings will take your place.
Once more your image will be left in the garden of love..

<u>Confused</u>

I am confused – for today the road is clear
    tomorrow debris every where.

I am confused – for today my eyes see beauty
    tomorrow the picture is messy.

I am confused – for today I am standing firmed
    tomorrow I may fall

I am confused – for today I am very happy
    tomorrow covered with misery.

I am confused – for today everything goes well
    tomorrow reality seems so far away

I am confused – for today I prayed to my God
    tomorrow the devil steps in.

Deceased

Journey through time has ended
some long – some short –
some rough – some smooth –
traveling through the day and in the night
in the rain and in the sun,
as the journey continues on

No more will you feel the wind lashing on your face
No more you will be soaked like the earth, for the rain has ceased.

No more pain and sorrow, for they comes not today nor to morrow,
No more tears running down your cheeks,
like a spring from beneath the earth's crust

No more disappointment, for you mind is at rest,
No more burden to bear, for your heart is at peace.
No more will you be tormented,
for your spirit has returned to its source.

Only Human

God could have made us like rocks and stones
But instead, He made us off flesh and bones,
He could have made us like trees and plants
Instead, He made us off complex body parts.

God could have made us like animals and birds
But instead, He made us guardians of His world,
He could have made us like snakes and reptiles
Instead, He made us to stand by His side
.
God could have made us like butterflies and bees
But instead, He made us with spirits and souls,
He could have made us like lakes and rivers
Instead, He made us His believers.

God could have made us like the breeze and the rain
But instead, He made as a human to feel pain,
He could have made us like the seas and fishes
Instead, He made us to sweat for our riches.

Peace

Peace is when the conscious mind and the subconscious mind
is in a state of equilibrium,
When the physical self and the spiritual self is in oneness,
Then, being will rejoice on the stage of creation.

The raging seas have no control over the moon,
The moon changes the behavior of all nature's creation on earth
Even the planets, obeys the terrestrial moon,
But mankind, God's creation
Possesses the supernatural power,
To control the wrought that invades the mind
And brings peace within his tempestuous Ego.

Knowledge

Is their light in a blind man's world ?
Or
Is their knowledge in a new born mind ?
For the light - the God maketh
For knowledge - the God giveth

If any man has not seen the light
Then, where is thy God ?
If any man is without knowledge
Then, where is thy God ?
For thy God is light and knowledge.

Crime

Crime has increased
The Holy book has spoken
Man turns beast
Crime will not decrease.

Children are indiscipline
Parents has failed
Souls lost in darkness
Caught in the devil's world.

Mankind has failed his purpose
To promote peace and righteousness
He has become a deserter
Betrayed the Creature's trust.

The Rebels

They walked this land without fear
Tormenting citizens with great terror,

Night and day they are lawless and ruthless
They crush everything that comes their way,

They would rub the rich and even the poor
Destroying properties, looting belongings,

They are an epidemic spreading through the land
Bringing fear and destruction wherever they go,

They honour and solute misery and pain
They bow before their God of destruction and doom,

They are heartless and brute-less worriers
And would kill anyone that comes in their path,

They are fanatic and uncontrollable bulls
Trampling in the field of hope and peace,

They would torment the souls of the young and the old
Bringing grief to their impetuous hearts,

They would takeaway the ecstatic joy from one's life
And replaces it with pains and sorrows,

The rebels are walking all over the land
Bringing fear and terror to its people,

The rebels are walking all over the land
It's timer the law needs to put a hand

Leave Me Alone

Leave me alone
Don't harass me
I know what I 'm doing
Just look and see.

Leave me alone
Don't disturb me
I can think clearly
Just watch –hold your peace.

Leave me alone
Don't provoke me
I'm not stupid
Just look – watch – hold your peace

Neighbors

Neighbors are good
Neighbors are bad
Some make you happy
Others make you sad.

Neighbors are honest
Neighbors are a disgrace
Some like family
Others like enemy.

Neighbors are damn-fast
Neighbors mind their business
Some lives happy
Other lives in misery

Where is Love

If we look around
what will we see ?
happiness in the home,
has broken down completely,
Fathers and Mothers
quarreling each night and day,
and their children following in their way

If we look around
what will we see ?
humans living dishonestly ,
discipline has eroded into the sea of sins.
every where we turn it's bad living.

If we look around we will observe
love has gone,
something is wrong,
something is wrong
Brothers and Sister, something is wrong,
Will we allow this to go on ?

Together to a brighter tomorrow

Together to a brighter tomorrow
May it be joy or may it be sorrow,
Let us unite and stand strong
Let peace and love be our song.

Together to a brighter tomorrow
We got to hold tight and don't let go,
Brothers and Sisters we got to work hand in hand
For a better nation and a better land.

Together to a brighter tomorrow
Let's think deep and not shallow,
Peace, love and happiness depends on us
Regardless of our color, religion or status.

Together to a brighter tomorrow
Our journey may be long or narrow
With hope and faith we will be through
You depend on me and I depends on you.

Music

Heart filled with love
Mind free from hate.

Thoughts are cleaner
Life is better.

Spirit vibrates
Body relates.

Body relax
Stresses delete.

Heart and mind meet
Music really sweet.

Glory of the Poui

The dry season has now begun
despite the rain drops now and then
The miraculous poui
distinguish itself by its awesome blossom –
yellow bells - pink bells -
but most outstanding of them all,
the tree that shines like the golden sun.

From a distance one can see its eloquent beauty
displayed by nature, upon a tree:

Yellow bells –
Pink bells –
Glitters like the sunset on the silver sea.

Yellow bells –
Pink bells –
Manifestation of nature's existence.

How you think so you live

Man who thinks of good things
Builds a fortress of love
Will receive many blessings
From the maker from above.

Man who thinks of bad things
Will inherit troubles
His mind intoxicated with sin
And duels among the devils

Man who thinks of himself
Knows not of unity
His gains are of selfishness
And dumb to reality.

Man who thinks of today
Leaves nothing for tomorrow
Will soon fads away
In misery and sorrow.

<u>**We are one**</u>

The same God who made you made me
Why live in hate and envy?
It's no use living our lives this way
Lets hold hands, sing and pray.

We all are from one home – planet earth
Regardless of our riches and fame we have the same worth
Unit, peace and love are life best qualities
Let's refrain from polluting our minds with iniquities.

We got to take care of our lives and our earth
In order to promote good health and proper growth
We got the brain to think and to reason
And the opportunity to go to heaven.

Let's live as one happy family
When someone is in need, always ready to help
Let love be the adhesive that binds us together
Don't let hate separate us from each other.

Woman

Without you this world would be incomplete
So don't let no man trample you under his feet
Let him know you have the rights to live and love
And is guided by the Father from above.

You are the most precious thing in the world
That man needs to cherish, love and hold
You give comfort and joy, pleasure after toil
Lift your head up high, for in man's world you are all.

You are the beauty and inspiration on earth's life
Everything in your name is worth the sacrifice
You're the diamond and gold, ruby and pearl
That man will fight and kill, to conquer with his
heart and soul.

Woman ! the whole world depends on you
Generation after generation will do the things you do
So let your voice echo through the distance of time
Stand-up for you rights and let no man corrupt your mind.

Mother

I will never forget the day I was born
When you took me in your arms and kept me warm
And when ever I screamed and cried
You will rock me in your arms and sing lullaby.

Although I was wretched and naughty at times
You protected me from dangers of any kind
You taught me to be patience and true
And now I am proud to say –
"Mother I honestly Love you"

O Mother you are so precious to me
If ever I hurt you, I'm sorry
Thanks to the good Lord from heaven above
For giving me a Mother with lots of love.

Just Yesterday

Just yesterday you was with us
Gracing us with your laughter and smiles
Just yesterday you was right here
With great moments of joy and pride.

Just yesterday the angels took you away
Leaving us with grief and sorrow
Just yesterday you silently said goodbye
See you all in Heaven tomorrow.

Today ! we embraces you with love
We honour you with gratitude
We adore you with sincerity.

We thank you for your patience
We thank you for your kindness
We thank you for sharing your joy and warmth
and showing us the road to righteousness.

Just yesterday – you was here
But today – yesterday has gone.

<u>Waiting</u>

In the hot sun
The line is long
In front of me
There are many
       -restless souls
       -frustrated souls
       -impetuous souls
Moving hands
Unstill feet
Heads bowed
Can't stand the heat
       -angry people
       -vex people
       -disgruntled people
Line moving slow
Should I stay or go?
Time is running out
Should I stay quite or shout?
       -dissatisfied voices
       -noisy voices
       -confused voices
The line is long
Should I stay?
Or
Should I go?

That's Life

Life is sour, Life is sweet
Be good to all you meet

Life is bad, Life is good
Live right is the way we should

Life is sickness, Life is death
Live each day without regret.

Life is sadness, Life is happiness
Be proud to ask forgiveness

Life is today, Life is tomorrow
Put aside our anger and sorrow

Life is lies, Life is honesty
 Aim for good health and prosperity

Life is hate, Life is love
Peace is in GOD above.

Book

I turned each page one by one
Read each line one after the other
Some are short others are long
I discovered from cover to cover.

Great names like Christ, Gandhi and King
And dates of birth and of death
Things I will always remember
Things my mind will never forget.

Love and joy, sorrow and hate
Things to laugh and things to cry
Men of courage and men of faith
Brave and strong, never too shy.

Words I will never erase
So many good things there-in
Words that brings such good taste
I read them all within.

A Lucky Day

It was a beautiful day in January
That will always live in my memory,
May be, the Lord has put it this way
For in my heart you will always stay.

Being with you I will always adore
Will like to live, to love you much more,
For the little time we may be together
You my Love, my heart will remember.

My love for you comes from within
Without you it's hard to go on living.
Each day my heart beats your name
Living together will never be in vain

Moving On

Today I am here
tomorrow; don't know where.

I'm young, I'm strong
power to move on.

No time to waste
I got to move in grace.

So much to accomplish
so much I wish.

Journey may be long
never to turn around.

Obstacles every where
regardless I will be there.

My faith is strong
no one to push me down.

My goals are clear
like wind in my ear.

My taste is sweet
like sugar between teeth.

My eyes are bright
like planet Venus at night.

I have courage, I have pride
destiny always at my side.

Abortion Satan's Way

Woman conceived - "with child"
The scriptures speak – many times
For an unborn or a newborn babe
Is no difference – but the same kind

We can call Him or Her – fetus or embryo
An infant which may not see the light
Like a seed planted – yet no chance to grow
Deprives from the rain and the sun light.

In the womb – secrets of earth are hidden
Waits the opportunity to be sanctified
Without doubt – there is no good reason
No one on earth can proudly justified.

Woman! don't let your fruit depart
Let no mischief evades your mind
For punishment will follow your path
Hope and love, search and you will find.

Innocent blood shall not be shed
The curse of God shall be upon you
The wicked ones condone death
The righteous will always be true.

God's work will always be forever
No one can destroy the soul
The body can be taken to the alter
But the soul dwells in God's world.

Woman! don't cover your self with shame
Standup for life-you will not regret
For the wrong- no one to be blame
The decision is yours – for life or death.

God has a plan for every newborn child
Born with life or born with death
Let the Lord spirit be your guide
Woman! No way will you ever regret.

The Fetus Speaks

Mummy! I am not dead
I know when you are angry.
I know when you are happy
Your emotions – I feel them
Your sadness -I taste them
Your tears bring sorrow
Your smiles bring joy.

Mummy! when you speaks
I feel the vibrations
When you're in pain
My heart cries.
Wherever you goes
My feet walk with you
When ever you sings
My heart sings with you

Mummy! I'm not dead
Every breathe you take
I take one too
Every sip you taste
My lips taste them too.

Mummy! when you're sleep
I am also asleep
When ever you dream
I dream with you.

Mummy! I am not a mistake
I am God's plan
For one day - one joyful day
I will see the light of the sun.

Fear of Evil

Where do we run
Where do we go
Where do we hide
from the criminals.

Who wants to be shot
Who wants a bulletin their heart
Who wants to feel the agony
of ripping flesh.

Fear of evil
Pollutes the environment
Fear of evil
Like a aura
hanging over our head.

Where do we run
Where do we go
Where do we hide
For the fear of evil
surrounds us.
Fear of evil

Like dark clouds
blocking the light of the sun
Fear of evil
affects everyone.

Tears

My heart is heavy
busting with tears
not only of sadness
but joy as well.

My heart is heavy
like passing clouds
and rolling thunder
brings memories
of joyful moments
brings memories
of sadness as time goes by.

Tears of happiness
tears of sadness
they are my tears.

Illusion

I heard the sound of drums
When I looked – there was on drums,
I heard chanting voices in the air
I looked – no one was there.

I heard footsteps coming towards me
When I looked – there was no feet,
I heard branches swaying in the wind
I looked – the place was still.

I smelled the flavor of curried – chicken
But when I looked - there was no kitchen,
I inhaled the aroma of old aged wine
But there was nothing of its kind.

I heard noise from clapping hands
But where are the hands ?
I heard someone calling my name
When I looked – I looked in vain.

I heard the sound of drums
I heard voices in the air
I heard foot steps coming
I heard branches swaying
I smelled curried – chicken
I inhaled old aged wine
I heard clapping hands
I heard someone calling
But when I looked
No one was there
I stood in despair.

Step by Step

As I climb along life' pathway
There will be obstacles in the way
I will not give-up, but will continued on
Turning back will be wrong.

One step at a time
Others will follow behind
One step forward
Is one step to reality
One step backward
Is one step to impudicity

One step today
One step tomorrow
As I journey through life's pathway
It may be joy or it may be sorrow.

Step by step
Regardless of failure
Or regardless of success
I will lift my head to the sky
For I know, I honestly tried.

Step by step
One day will take you to the top.

Possess

The young woman came at the alter
Jumping, shaking – calling names in different tongues
The congregation stood in despair
While the preacher and elders try to calm her down.

"What evil spirits beheld her", the preacher murmured
She possess the strength of seven lions
She kicked and wrestled with great power
Over-coming seven righteous men.

The ramping and kicking went on for several hours
Until the preacher made contact the evil spirits
She lied still, sweat running like water from a spring
As the words from the preacher purified and transmuted her.

The preacher and his elder-men cast the spirits away
In her heart, it was like a new day
She stood in amazement, wondering what went wrong
When she heard the congregation singing " Jesus shall overcome"

The preacher and his elders took her to her countryside home
And gathered the family to worship and to pray
Then he bestowed God's blessings from room to room
Hoping the evil spirits will not come back too soon.

The Sea

Sometimes you are rageous like a lion
Sometimes you are splendid and charm
Regardless how rageous or charm you may be
You are the source of life to all humanity.

Your behaviour we can tell by the moon
Whether morning, noon or night
Whenever we go to fish or swim
You bring great joy and sometimes sadness within.

Ships sail from island to island
Transporting cargo, goods of all kind
Though it may take many days
You are so useful in many ways.

Fishes, crabs, snails and other sea creatures
Living beneath your crystal blue waters
Chorals, plant, minerals and precious stones
Man dives at you depth, brave and alone.

You are three times the size of earth's land
In our atlas – colourful maps we can find
Deep and shallow, wide and narrow
Your surface reflects a thousand shadows.

The Vagrant

On the road, street or in the park
May it be morning, noon or the dark
With ragged clothes and shaggy hair
From here to there with nothing to care.

Dirty, stink and ugly they may be
They live day by day tax -free
No water rate, electricity nor phone bills to pay
Cost of living does not affect them in anyway.

Sometimes they may be happy or sad
Some behave good others play mad
No one knows when they may attack
So be aware and don't turn your back.

It makes no sense laughing at them
Instead let's put a hand and try to help them
For we don't know when the table may turn
Let us patiently watch and learn.

I Am Leaving (1966)

A message came
Like a bandit at night
I felt hopeless and insane
Sleep took its last flight.

Preparation began
News spread like wildfire
On faces sadness shone
Willing to fulfill my desire.

Leaving my beautiful home
Hurtful decision to be made
First time I will be all alone
Strict rules were made.

It was goodbye and farewell
Sad and happy faces
I love them all so well
Soon I will be in strange places.

On my enthusiastic journey
I thought of heaven and hell
Prayers were my testimonies
Spirit vibrations meant well.

A Blind Man's World

I cannot see
but I know
when the sun is up
and when night falls.

I can smell
the freshness of the wind
and knows the terror when it rain

I know when young lovers
are reminiscing under the moon
and owls and bats come-out
not too soon.

I cannot see
yet my world it not dark
my hands and feet guides me-
not only to the edge
but to my destiny.

I can smell the aroma of good food
and knows what lies in the bin.

I can taste the bitterness of one's life
yet I know the moment of joy
and happiness of the heart.

I cannot see
yet my mind displays images around
my brains manifest it's self
in my *being*

<u>Forgiveness</u>

When someone hates you and do you wrong things
Let your reaction, be not that of hate
Take the key of love- open the mind's gate
And let the good things escape from within

It makes no sense fighting, just stop and think
It's no use substituting hate for hate
Doing wrong not going to make you grate
So open your eyes to the good things.

When wicked action parades the mind plain
Nothing good the ego can comprehend
Sickness and suffering it's all can be gained
Bring our sinful lives to an end.

We must forgive each other for the wrong
Leave the bad things behind –
Let truth continue on.

Journey Of Hope

I lived so many times again and again
Each time I promised to be better and better
Here I am weak and foolish instead
Now I am to do it all over again.

This time I have a master plan
To satisfy my restless mind
I don't want to go over again and again
There is little to loose and much to gain.

I am challenging my self once more
My master plan is very sure
I will remove the mistakes
from past (years)
And wash my hopes with life's golden tears.

Tanka 1

A beautiful day?
suddenly! heavy rain came
many homes flooded
emergency came in time
innocent lives have been saved.

Tanka 2

Words of syllables
make spelling very easy
large words or small ones
combination of great sounds
satisfaction to poets.

Haiku 1

Worm digs through the soil
lizard follows its journey
life suddenly ends.

Haiku 2

Election time comes
many promises are made
voters bow in shame.

A Wonderful World.

What a wonderful world You has given us?
With all it's glories we can see
Beautiful rivers, mountains and trees
Even flowers fruits and seeds.

What a unique world You has made
And it's wonders such as night and day
Beautiful rain, wind and earth of clay
Even the moon, sun and stars in the milky- way.

What a planet of all planets?
With different types of climates
Beautiful people of all colour and race
Knowledge of love, hope and grace.

What a universe that's so designed?
Placing trust in the bosom of mankind
Mankind has betrayed the trust
What was started will soon come to an ends

Children Are Dying

Drought and famines
Through out earth's land
Children are starving
Lord! put a hand.

The rain has eloped
On the wings of the wind
There is no hope
Children are suffering.

The sun comes out in it's glory
Looking down on the parched earth
Children are in agony
Wish there were no birth.

Drought and famines
Through out earth's land
Children are dying
Lord! Please put a hand.

Cane Cutters

in the rain
in the sun
they worked
from dust to dawn.

they were all wet
from head to feet
but continued on
cutting cane
as they move along.

sore hands
wearied feet
they continued
regardless of the pain
cutting cane
in the sun
in the rain.

clothes painted black
hands and feet are the same
this did not held them back
from moving on
cutting cane
in the rain
in the sun
men and women
cutting cane
from dust to dawn.

Different Life

Man and Woman
living in the world
with love and hate.

Man and Woman
living in a world
with right and wrong.

Man and Woman
have the opportunity
to choose what is good
and what is bad-
yet some will choose that which is of evil
for there is pleasure in it -
and the good they left behind
for there is no joy for them.

For those who chosen the good
the world is still beautiful
despite the evils that prevails
for they find hope and comfort
in their Saviour .

The Sun Light

The mist elopes with the morning wind
dark clouds partly covered the sky
It's dim light emits from beyond
showing a faint expression
on the soft surface on the horizon.

The rays penetrated through the black clouds
landing on earth's green jacket
the wet crust gradually dries
leaving a smooth clean surface.

Dark clouds suddenly disappeared
golden sun with its white background
sunlight filled earth's atmosphere
darkness hiding, cannot be found.

The Roadside Fisherman

Stall by the road side
Easy to catch the eyes
As people passes by
Easy to sell-
Easy to smell-

Dead fish sleeping on counter
Big and small-
Side by side-
Like dead soldiers
Harassed by angry flies.

As daybreak erased by the morning sun
The fisherman turns the sprinkler on
Stale fish becomes fresh
Dead fish becomes alive-
"Fresh fish, Fresh fish" He sings
Weighing them on the rusty scale
As customers awaits their turn.

The Push Cart

As morning breaks it's way,
Under the faded light of the sun
Squeaking sounds
Travel on the wave of the cool breeze
Signaling the coming of the push cart
Journeying to it's destiny-
The market place
No goods to carry
No goods to bring
Empty bottles gesture the morning hymn
Rum bottles-
Bear bottles-
Specially selected
Fletches the best price
As the push cart makes it's way
To the buyer.

PART TWO

Virgin Mary

God's chosen one
Conceived by the Holy Spirit
The Power of God
Unto Mary it came

Joseph was angry
Knowing Mary with baby
An angel came
Peace was made.

The Birth of Jesus

Joseph and Mary went on their way
Looking for a place to stay,
For the moment was at hand
A place they must find.

In the stable they spend the night
What an unusual sight?
Their bed was made of hay
Holy Babe to lead the way.

Three wise men came from afar
In the sky they saw a bright star,
Which lead them to the manger,
A place free from danger.

Thank you Lord

Thank you Lord
for the beautiful earth
all its values and its worth.

Thank you Lord
for the clouds in the sky
birds and bees and all that fly

Thank you Lord
for the land, water, and air
ozone layer in the atmosphere

Thank you Lord
for the moon and the stars
planets Venus, Jupiter, and Mars.

Thank you Lord
for the sun and the rain
the fields and the grains.

Thank you Lord
the fishes in the sea
and all its beauty one can see.

Thank you Lord
for the rivers and the mountains
pretty flowers and crystal springs.

Thank you Lord
for the animals and the plants
all insects, even the ants.

Thank you Lord
for man and woman
that you placed on earth's land.

Thank you Lord
for we can laugh and sing
regardless the troubles life bring.

Thank you Lord
for we can weep and sleep
know all things sour and sweet.

Thank you Lord
for the sorrow and the pains
blood that flows in our veins.

Thank you Lord
for the strength and wisdom
and your glorious kingdom.

Thank you Lord
for showing us the way
journeying through the night and day.

Thank you Lord
for body, spirit, and soul
opportunity to enter your world.

The son of God

The son of God
Who came to earth
Proclaiming His faith
To all mankind.

The son of God
Came as a mortal being
Stood-up to temptation
Suffered on a cross.

The son of God
Demonstrated true love
Gave His life
For all sinners.

The son of God
Promised to come again
To delivered us
From the evil souls.

The Children's Prayer

Lord God I pray your blessings upon our children
Protect them from the evils that surround them
Guide them into the path of righteousness
Heal them from the wounds of physical and spiritual abuse
Lead them into a world of honesty and love
Show them the way to heaven's gate
Teach them to care, to love, and have courage to live
Mould them O lord so they can grow into your garden of divinity
Strengthen them that they will withstand the pressures of life
Feed them with knowledge so they can attained transcendental bliss
Forgive them for all their mistakes for they no not what they have done
Don't depart from them, I beg you Lord
For without you they are weak –
Without you they are lost in hopelessness
Lord God I pray, be with them all the way- every day.
Thank You Lord.

The Great One

The Promised Messiah
Eternal and Divine One
Was sent by His Father
To preach the Gospel to every one

The Promised Messiah
Filled with Divine Grace
Was sent by His Father
To save the human race

The Promised Messiah
Filled with the Holy Ghost
Was sent by His Father
To washed man's sins away

The Promised Messiah
Spiritual and Holy One
Was sent by His Father
To save us from Satan

The Promised Messiah
Son of the true and Living God
Was sent by His Father
To teach us to forgive and to love

Adam and Eve

God made me so true
Out off me -
He then made you,
He made us both
to live as one,
For I'm the Man
You're the Woman.

God made you and me
To live in love and harmony,
Disobedience bought us shame
Satan proclaimed his name.

Troubles we have to bear
We cannot run or hide anywhere.

I Gave Myself To Thee

I gave myself to thee
In order to live free
Living in the way of troubles
Enslave me in a world of evils.

I gave myself to thee
So happiness will follow me
For there are no good things
Living in a world of sins.

I gave myself to thee
So good things will follow me
True life I will always live
Good things I will always give.

I give myself to thee
Thee alone can set me free
Free from earth's problems
Don't matter how big- He can solve them.

I give myself to thee
For in thee I will always be free
The Lord is my way and light
In Him everything will be alright.

I give myself to thee
Protected I will be
All through the night and day
I will be protected in every way.

Guidance

O my heavenly Father
I am your sheep
Protect me from the loins
While I lay in sleep.

My Love For You

Love in my hear
Peace in my soul
Christ I'll never part
Heaven is my goal.

Love in my mind
Power in my spirit
I will walk hand in hand
Christ being my prophet.

Jesus -The Now

How long can we live in sin?
It will destroy our minds deep within
For with Satan, we'll always suffer
Life will vanish forever.

How long can we live in sin?
The disease that feeds on our being
Evil will follow wherever we go
Satan will devour our egos.

Now long can we live sin?
It's time to clean our hearts within
Let Jesus come into our blood
Our hearts will fill with eternal love.

Bless Ye The Children

Bless ye the little children
For they are so precious to us
Keep them away from Satan's den
So they can worship thee
Dear Lord! Dear Lord!
Keep them safe with thee.

Forgive ye the little children
For they are tender and carefree
Fill them with your righteousness
So they can praise thee
Dear Lord! Dear Lord!
Let them grow with thee.

Protect ye the little children
For they are helpless and weak
Spread your love around them
So they will know thee
Dear Lord! Dear Lord!
You're their guide.

Praise ye the little children
For they are you creation
Open their hearts to your spirit
So they can know your true love
Dear Lord! Dear Lord!
Take them into your kingdom.

I Sing A Song

I sing a song, I sing a song
As I toiled from dust to dawn
I sing a song, I sing a song
For you O Lord I sing a song.

Jesus Love You

Jesus loves you, Jesus loves you
In spite all the wrong things you do
Jesus loves you, Jesus loves you
He wants you to love Him too.

Seeking The Lord

My Lord! My Lord!
I come to thee
My Lord! My Lord!
I want to be free.

My Lord! My Lord!
On bending knees
My Lord! My Lord!
I confess to thee.

My Lord! My Lord!
My heart cries in pain
My Lord! My Lord!
Let my cries not be in vain.

My Lord! My Lord!
Fill me with your joy
My Lord! My Lord!
Lift me in your love.

My Lord! My Lord!
I need you by my side
My Lord! My Lord!
My longing for you *will never die.*

What A Way O Lord

A journey so long
A road so rough
What a way O Lord
That is so tough.

A distance so long
A faith so weak
What a way O Lord
Your hope I seek.

A way so long
Courage has gone
What a way O Lord
This is my song.

A path so long
I can't go no more
What a way O Lord
I need you for sure.

Jesus Love You

Jesus loves you, Jesus loves you
In spite all the wrong things you do
Jesus loves you, Jesus loves you
He wants you to love Him too.

Jesus Called Us Again

Jesus called us again
To assemble in His name
With fellowship with one another
Despite our races or cultures.

Jesus called us again
To worship in His name
With love, peace, and unity
In His name we'll be free.

Jesus called us again
Nothing in His name shall be in vain
Our spirit He will elevate
In heaven He sits and wait.

Jesus The Man

Jesus the man
Born from a virgin
Suffered on a cross
Die for our sins
Jesus the man
We called King of Kings.

Jesus the man
Who shows us the way
Thought us to love
And live in righteousness
Jesus the man
We called Lord of Lord.

Jesus the man
Who performed many miracles
Healed the sick
Care for the weak and the poor
Jesus the man
We called Master of the world.

Jesus the man
Who was sent by God
Lovers of all sinners
Teacher of all nations
Jesus the man
We called Emmanuel.

The Last Moment

I am sorry for the things I have done
And now I am trying , trying to run
Run from the wickedness of this world
To save my spirit and my soul…
Now I am crying, O Lord! O Lord!
For the earth is open with fire all around
O Lord! O Lord! I cried!
Please don't let me die.

I never obeyed the rules of the Lord
Never tried to live a life in His way
Now the beat of my heart brings sadness
How long will I lived?
How long will I die?
I am pleading O Lord! O Lord!
 For the earth is open with fire all around
O Lord! O Lord! I cried!
Please don't let me die.

I turned my back from the trueness of life
And cling to hate, never think twice
The time has come to pay for the wrong
For there is no time, no time to wait…
I am earning for you O Lord! O Lord!
For the earth is open with fire all around
O Lord! O Lord I cry!
please don't let me die

All In One

One God
One Master
One Creator
That made me
 -The Man
One Body
One Soul
One Spirit
To do the things
As best as I can
As was told
By
One God
One Master
One Creator

Open My Eyes

Open my eyes to your world, dear Lord
So that I may see thy works there in
I may learn to live and love, dear Lord
And cherish this life of yours that's within.

Open my heart to your life, dear Lord
And let the blood of goodness flows
That I may be strong in you, dear Lord
To live among my friends and foes.

Open my mind to your Spirit, dear Lord
That I may honor you each day
To do the things for you, dear Lord
So that I may be with you some day.

It's Good To Know You Lord

It's good to know you Lord
Wherever I may go
When ever I am in need
Your name is all I know.

It's good to know you Lord
For the joy in my life
Now sorrow exists no more
All to you I sacrifice.

All For Jesus

I will clap my hands for Jesus,
I will clap my hands for Jesus,
I will clap my hands for Jesus,
For Jesus is my only way.

I will sing a song for Jesus,
I will sing a song for Jesus,
I will sing a song for Jesus,
For Jesus is my guide.

I will stand up for Jesus,
I will stand up for Jesus,
I will stand up for Jesus,
For Jesus is my everlasting life.

He Is Right Here

I walked a mile
Day after day
I walk
For thy love-
I hope
I pray
God I search
Only to know
Only to find
He is right here
Within my soul
Within my heart.

Lost In Hope

I'm alone and despair
With troubles around about:
No one I can see or hear
It's no use trying to shout.

I just have to hope and pray
For my faith to be strong
Hoping some one will come my way
This I know not- how long.

Where are you O Lord
Make known thy self to me
Show me just once my Lord
A way to be forever free.

Good Morning! Dear Lord

Good morning, good morning dear Lord
Thanks for this life once more
Good morning, good morning dear Lord
Your name I praise and adore.

<u>Together</u>

Together we are in the Lord
Together we are one
Together we live in love
Together we mighty strong.

Together we sing praises (to the Lord)
Together we kneel in prayer
Together we will live in unity
And promote life's dignity

In The Beginning

In the beginning God made the world
With many trees and birds
He even made the fishes in the seas
Plants, flowers and the bees

He created the animals and the snakes
And the beautiful rivers and the lakes
He even made the moon, sun and stars
Distance planets such as Saturn and mars.

He took clay and made a man
Placed him in a beautiful land
With no worries and no fear
Free to roam every where.

He gave him power to choose what is right
Protected him during the day and night
He even made him an adorable companion
Placed them both in the garden of Eden.

I Thirst

My lips are dried
I whispered
I cried
Like a babe
Like a child
For the freedom
of humanity
I thirst
I cried
A world so sad.

Our Creator

Who made the earth and all the trees?
Animals, birds and fishes in the seas

Who made the rain and sun to shine?
Created man in the image of His kind

Who made true love to conquer hate?
Gave us Jesus, the key to heaven's gate.

Who awaits in Heaven high above?
It's the one and only -Eternal GOD.

Touch Me

Touch me in the morning
Touch me in the evening
Touch me Lord, touch me
Touch me with your spirit.

Touch me while I am walking
Touch me while I am sleeping
Touch me Lord, touch me
Touch me with your spirit

Touch me in my thinking
Touch me in my doings
Touch me Lord, touch me
Touch me with your spirit

I Pray

I pray for health
And not for wealth-

I pray for the weak
For strength they seek-

I pray for the sick
And their healing quick-

I pray for the children
And their guidance-

I pray for the world
And all its evil souls.